Five Plays
From The Gospels

The Wedding Feast At Cana
The Meeting In Bethany
I Will Send You Elijah
Pilate
The First Easter

By Karl F. Hollenbach

NOTICE:

The Author, Karl F. Hollenbach, has authorized royalty-free performances of any or all of these *Five Plays From The Gospels* as long as no alterations are made to the intent of the subject matter.

Createspace ISBN: 0615733891
Createspace ISBN-13: 978-0615733890

ACKNOWLEDGEMENTS

The author and publisher, internet marketing KY, LLC gratefully acknowledge the tremendous assistance of our Book Publicist, Charles T Franklin, whose professional knowledge of online book publishing made the second publishing of these plays possible.

Additionally the author and publisher wish to acknowledge the focused and timely work of our transcriptionist, Elenie Hernandez, and proofreader, Mary Martin.

The front cover image is from the Alaverdi Gospels (1054)
Description: English: "the Alaverdi Gospels" written in the Georgian nuskhuri script.
The manuscript (A-484) was copied by the Georgian monks on the Black Mountain in Syria and then kept at the Alaverdi convent in Georgia.

File Title:
The Alaverdi Four Gospels 1054 St. Matthew the Evangelist and the Gospel's Title-Page

Page URL:
http://commons.wikimedia.org/wiki/File%3AAlaverdi_Gospels_(1054).jpg

File URL:
http://upload.wikimedia.org/wikipedia/commons/6/62/Alaverdi_Gospels_%281054%29.jpg

Attribution:
See page for author [Public domain], via Wikimedia Commons. .

The Living Jesus

PREFACE

These five one-act plays were written to be performed before a Sunday School class or during a church service. "The Wedding Feast at Cana" was performed at St. Andrew United Church of Christ in 2001 and at Brandenburg United Methodist Church in 2006. "The Meeting at Bethany", "Pilate", and "The First Easter" were performed at Brandenburg United Methodist Church during the succeeding three years.

The plot of each play derives from an instance from the Gospels but is influenced by the frequent comments by Jesus, that he had come to preach the Kingdom of Heaven, and by historical references to Jesus' travels in India.

The photograph of the living Jesus on the preceding page replaced the crucified image on the Turin Shroud with the risen Jesus in color. In like manner these five plays replace the Christmas and Easter myths about Jesus with the message of Jesus, that the Kingdom of Heaven, which is here and now and within, should be sought first, it being "The Pearl of Great Price".

Karl F. Hollenbach

PREAMBLE

All of the biblical passages within the appendix helped Karl F. Hollenbach to personalize the dialogue of the characters within the 5 plays so the strength of the message of Christ and the Kingdom of Heaven show through the writing. It is intended to illustrate the central focus of the work, which is the "message, not the messenger" attitude with which Christ lived, delivered his sermons, and died for our sins on the cross.

- Publisher

TABLE OF CONTENTS

THE LIVING JESUS   iii

A visitor to Sai Baba's Ashram in Puttaparti, India had with her a crucifix and a black-and-white photo of the image of Christ from the Turin Shroud, which she hoped the Baba would bless for her. Sai Baba looked at the items held out for his blessing and refused to accept the crucifix. With a lift and wave of his hand, he drew the black-and-white image of Christ from the photograph until there was nothing but a blank sheet of gloss photo paper. He then drew up and through that blank sheet the image seen on this photograph: that of the risen Jesus in color.

PREFACE   iv

PREAMBLE   v

TABLE OF CONTENTS   vi

1   THE WEDDING FEAST AT CANA   1

2   THE MEETING IN BETHANY   13

3   I WILL SEND YOU ELIJAH   27

4   PILATE   38

5   THE FIRST EASTER   50

APPENDIX   62

ABOUT THE AUTHOR   67

Karl F. Hollenbach

THE WEDDING FEAST AT CANA

NARRATOR

Our play takes place in Cana at the sumptuous home of David, a relative of Mary and her son Jesus, who has just recently been baptized by John. As our play opens, Mary and Jesus have entered the gardens of David's home. Mary speaks to Jesus.

MARY

"There is our cousin David by those two columns. I doubt that he recognizes you, Jesus. It has been years since he last saw you."

JESUS

"I recognize him, Mother."

MARY

"He's talking with his young nephew, Judas. Judas is a bright young man. After his father died, David provided Judas with a fine education. David sees us now. He's coming over."

DAVID

"Mary! Mary! I am so glad to see you. I appreciate your willingness to act as mistress of my home today for Mariam's wedding. With my dear Sarah dead these past two years, I am at a loss to see that everything goes well for my daughter's wedding feast."

MARY

"I am honored to be of help to you and Mariam, David. Do you not remember Jesus?"

DAVID

"Cousin! How long has it been since you left Galilee?"

JESUS

"Ten years."

DAVID

"You have grown to full manhood, Jesus. It is good to see you again. I am so glad you brought him with you, Mary."

MARY

"When he heard that Mariam was getting married, I had no trouble convincing him to take a day from his travels and come to her wedding feast with me."

DAVID

"Yes. Mariam will be pleased to see you, Jesus. You must go to her, Mary. She has been waiting for you. I shall have my chief steward take you to her. Heman! Heman, come here."

HEMAN

"Yes, Master."

DAVID

"Heman, this is my cousin Mary. You and the entire staff are to do whatever she bids you do. First, though, take her to your young mistress."

HEMAN

"Yes, Master. Please! Follow me, Mistress."

MARY

"I'll let Mariam know you are here, Jesus. She'll want to see you right away." (EXITS)

DAVID

"I have heard things about you, Jesus, since you've returned."

JESUS

"What have you heard, David?"

DAVID

"That you follow John."

JESUS

"John baptized me."

DAVID

"But you have not become a Nasserite as John has?"

JESUS

"No."

DAVID

"But you have become a Nazarene?"

JESUS

"Yes."

DAVID

"So you can marry but John the Nasserite cannot."

JESUS

(Laughs) "I can come to your daughter's wedding feast but John cannot."

DAVID

"I have been told that John said he should be baptized by you, but you said that it was proper that you be baptized by him."

JESUS

"Yes, that is right."

DAVID

"And that you are gathering disciples about you and that you have been going throughout Galilee preaching that God's Kingdom is coming."

JESUS

"I tell those that listen to me that the Kingdom of Heaven is here, now; within each of us."

DAVID

"Herod will tolerate no talk of kingdom in his domain, Jesus. And neither will Rome."

JESUS

"The Kingdom of Heaven is not of this world, David. It is not the world of Rome nor of Herod."

DAVID

"Ah! But will they understand that? Do you see that man taking a bunch of grapes from the table? That is Phinius. He is Herod's emissary. I do not doubt that he knows who you are and will seek you out soon. Be cautious. You will excuse me now? I have other guests to meet." (EXITS)

NARRATOR

David leaves Jesus. A moment later Mary and Heman come to Jesus. Anxiously Mary speaks.

MARY

"Now Heman, you are to do whatever he tells you. Jesus, Heman informs me that all four of the wine jars are empty and the wedding feast has not yet begun!"

JESUS

"What has that to do with me, Mother?"

MARY

"David is our cousin. This is Mariam's wedding. We cannot be out of wine! You're always helping others in need. Now your own family is in need."

JESUS

"Woman, my time has not yet come."

MARY

"It has now. You must do this out of charity and love for your cousin's reputation. Heman! You do everything he tells you to do. Do you understand? I have other things to attend to now. Remember, whatever he bids you do, you do!"

HEMAN

"Yes, Mistress."

NARRATOR

Mary leaves and Heman stands in front of Jesus waiting for some instruction.

JESUS

"Heman!"

HEMAN

"Yes, Master."

JESUS

"So you are the chief steward?"

HEMAN

"Yes, Master."

JESUS

"And the wine is your responsibility?"

HEMAN

"Yes, Master. I fear to tell Master David that there is no more wine. Whatever you can do to help …"

JESUS

"It seems God has expressed his will through my Mother."

HEMAN

"I do not understand, Master."

JESUS

"It doesn't matter, Heman. Whom have you told that there is no more wine left?"

HEMAN

"Only Mistress Mary, and, of course, you."

JESUS

"Then let us keep it among the three of us, Heman."

HEMAN

"Yes, Master. If you can help …."

JESUS

"Heman, can you obtain four jars of the sweet water from the well by the Roman Gate?"

HEMAN

"Master, I have only this morning had six new jars filled with the water from the well. They stand next to the empty wine jars in the storage room."

JESUS

"You have not cleaned the four empty wine jars?"

HEMAN

"No, Master. The jars are empty of wine and remain as they were, standing in the storage room. The insides still retain the red color and the jars still smell of wine."

JESUS

"Pour the fresh water from just four jugs into the empty wine jugs."

HEMAN

"To clean them, Master?"

JESUS

"No, Heman, so that the fresh water mixes with the red coloring and the smell of the wine which still lingers in the old wine jars."

HEMAN

"Master, it does not require four full jars of fresh water to clean out the wine jars."

JESUS

"You are not cleaning them with the fresh water, Heman. After you have filled each of the four empty wine jars, fill the wine bowls from them and begin serving the guests."

HEMAN

"I am to do whatever you tell me, Master. But Master David will deal harshly with me if I serve his guests water."

JESUS

"You will be serving them wine, Heman, and your Master David will be pleased with your efficiency."

HEMAN

"I shall do exactly as you say, Master."

NARRATOR

Heman leaves Jesus. Phinius, the Emissary of Herod, approaches. Phinius speaks.

PHINIUS

"Greetings, worthy teacher."

JESUS

"Greetings to you, noble Emissary."

PHINIUS

"I am only one of the guests today, as, I suppose, you are?"

JESUS

"I knew Mariam as a young child, many years ago. She is my cousin."

PHINIUS

"Yes, of course. (PAUSE) Herod, our king, has heard of your abilities."

JESUS

"What has that old fox heard?"

PHINIUS

"Herod may be old, but a fox he must be to continue to keep our Jewish law and traditions while we are under Roman rule. It is your ability to gather multitudes that interest him."

JESUS

"Is that all?"

PHINIUS

"Most esteemed teacher, you speak of the coming of God's kingdom. It is this kingdom for which Herod labors to bring to fruition under the protection of Roman rule. You can contribute to his vision. If I could tell him you would accept, he might offer you a position on his council."

JESUS

"We do not speak of the same kingdom, Phinius. My kingdom is not of this world."

PHINIUS

"Yes, yes, it is, as you teach, of the spirit."

JESUS

"It is the kingdom within. The more one concentrates on the outside, the less one will know of the inner glory of the everlasting joy of Spirit. The more one concentrates within, the less difficulties one has without."

PHINIUS

"And King Herod wishes to have fewer difficulties. Consider his offer."

JESUS

"You and Herod do not understand this truth because of your desire for worldly power. You have become engrossed in it and it does not allow you to think of deeper realities."

PHINIUS

"I shall inform King Herod that you are considering his offer."

JESUS

"Then you would be lying, Phinius."

PHINIUS

"King Herod is a generous man, Jesus. He can be most magnanimous to those who serve him. Do not waste your powers with the likes of that old hermit, John. I depart from you with this one suggestion: do not become an enemy of the king." (EXITS)

NARRATOR

"Phinius bows mockingly to Jesus and leaves. Mariam rushes to Jesus and throws her arms around his neck. She speaks."

MARIAM

"How wonderful to see you again, Jesus! You have been away far too long."

JESUS

"My dear child. You have become a young woman, a beautiful young woman. It does my heart good to see you again, Mariam. I am pleased to see you so happy, and glad that I am able to attend your wedding feast."

MARIAM

"You used to call me your 'Little Mariam.' You called me that even when I was eleven and you left us. I remember how you would surprise all of us children with flowers and sweets that magically poured from your outstretched hand."

JESUS

"Yes. When we are young we do foolish things."

MARIAM

"Your mother told me crowds gather throughout Galilee to hear you speak. Do you perform those surprises with your hands to gain their attention?"

JESUS

"I wish only to arouse in them the love of God. They should not be influenced by displays of unusual powers."

MARIAM

"Well, I enjoyed those displays you did for us children. I remember how pleased you made me when you would shake your hand and suddenly be holding a red rose, and you would give it to me for my hair."

JESUS

"But you have a red rose in your hair … now."

NARRATOR

Mariam places her right hand on her head. Jesus smiles and speaks.

JESUS

"On the other side, Mariam."

MARIAM

"How did it get there?"

JESUS

"A lovely young woman on her wedding day is granted her wish. God's blessing be upon you, my child."

MARIAM

"I must hurry back. It is so good to see you again, Jesus. I shall keep the rose." (EXITS)

NARRATOR

Mariam leaves Jesus. Judas approaches. He speaks.

JUDAS

"They are saying that my uncle has kept the best wine for last. But Heman informs me that you have saved him from the wrath of his master. I have heard of your powers, Jesus."

JESUS

"And what would that be, Judas?"

JUDAS

"I have not given you my name! How do you know it? Ah! A demonstration of your powers! Yes. I have heard about the lame man who now walks, the possessed child who is released from the demon, the blind beggar who now sees. And now wine from water! (PAUSE) You are familiar with the Zealots who plan the return of God's Kingdom?"

JESUS

"They are foolish children that play deadly games, Judas."

JUDAS

"Foolish? To live under the yoke of Roman rule is foolish. I saw that jackal Phinius talking with you. He is Herod's lackey. Be cautious. Herod stays in power only because he does the bidding of Caesar. The Zealots will soon bring about God's kingdom through a holy revolt and the Roman legions and that puppet Herod will be swept away."

JESUS

"You are a talented young man, Judas. If you wish to see the kingdom of Heaven, believe me, it will not be by joining the Zealots. Do not let the spirit of your higher thoughts be lost in flesh. The kingdom you are seeking is within, not without. Herod's throne, Caesar's empire will perish in time, but the Kingdom of Heaven will endure forever."

JUDAS

"I have spoken with Peter and Andrew."

JESUS

"They have become my disciples."

JUDAS

"They told me. They told me, and told me, and told me, as if they had had too much wine. They are simple men. They are uneducated men. While I …"

JESUS

"You are gifted, educated, and have the ability to be a leader of men, Judas. If those gifts lead you to search for the Kingdom of Heaven, then join me. Consider it. In one week, I leave for Capernium with those disciples I now have. David is motioning for me to come to him. Consider what I have said."

NARRATOR

Jesus leaves Judas and walks towards David. Judas thinks to himself.

JUDAS

"With his powers the people would make him their king and overthrow the Roman yoke that crushes us and divides us. If I join him, I could gradually persuade him away from the notion of his inner kingdom of which he speaks. I could force his hand; put him on the spot sometime, somewhere, so that he would have to use his powers. Those powers that Jesus has could overcome Rome and that kingly pretender, Herod and bring about God's kingdom on earth … now. If I am cunning and clever, I can force him to use his powers for that end. It is I who can make him king of Israel. I would be first among his followers. Why, I would be first among his disciples. And that is as it should be. I shall bide my time. I hear you O God of Israel! Your kingdom shall come, and I, Judas Iscariot, shall help bring it about."

NARRATOR

Jesus has walked over to where David is. David speaks to Jesus.

DAVID

"I told you Phinius would seek you out. I was pleased to see that my nephew Judas went to you, and that you spoke with him."

JESUS

"Your nephew is an ambitious young man."

DAVID

"And gifted with an excellent mind. I am concerned, however, that he is too clever and cunning for his own good. It would please me a great deal if he could be among your followers for a time and away from those Zealots who will only bring further destruction upon us."

JESUS

"If it is God's will."

DAVID

"The procession to the wedding feast is about to begin, Jesus. I am going to escort your mother. Mariam wishes you to escort her to the table next to her future husband and his family."

JESUS

"I am honored. This will be a joyous day to remember. Here, Mariam, take my arm. May God bless this union and give you peace and happiness for all your life."

NARRATOR

A secret tradition says that the spirit of Judas Iscariot appeared three hundred years later as the great Roman Emperor Constantine, who in 325 AD, made Christianity the official religion of the Roman Empire.

THE MEETING IN BETHANY

CHARACTERS:
John the Baptist
Lazarus
Mary
Martha
Jesus
Joseph of Arimathea, Narrator

PLACE: Home of Lazarus and his sisters in Bethany
TIME: Shortly after the baptism of Jesus

JOSEPH OF ARIMATHEA

I am Joseph. Joseph of Arimathea. You will know me later as the man who placed Jesus' body in the new tomb that was hewn out of the rock for me. I am a disciple of Jesus now. I say now, because … but our play will reveal that.

We are in Bethany, which is a small village just east of Jerusalem in Judea. Jesus' cousins, Lazarus and Lazarus' two sisters, Martha and Mary, live here. Lazarus and Martha are working in their garden, talking. Lazarus is speaking of John, their cousin, who is sometimes called John the Baptizer.

LAZARUS

"Here, Martha, let me help you with that bale before John arrives."

MARTHA

"I can handle it myself, Lazarus. You move the rest of those jugs. There isn't enough time to prepare everything. Why didn't Andrew tell you sooner?"

LAZARUS

"Martha! Martha! Do not be so anxious. Andrew didn't tell me sooner because John told him only yesterday."

MARTHA

"That John would meet Jesus … here? … Today?"

LAZARUS

"Yes, Martha. Andrew told me that the old fox King Herod has his spies looking for John."

MARTHA

"What about John's disciples? Aren't they in danger from Herod's grasp?"

LAZARUS

"King Herod expects no problem from John's followers once he has John's head. John's disciples want him to remain safe in the wilderness, but John insists that he meet with Jesus once again. That's why John is secretly coming here, Andrew told me."

MARTHA

"There just isn't enough time! Mary! Come out here and help me."

LAZARUS

"She's making something special for Jesus, Martha. She's young and you know how she idolizes him."

MARTHA

"Young? She's only five years younger than I am. She's "idle" for sure and lets me do all the work. Mary?"

JOSEPH OF ARIMATHEA

"Mary comes out of the house."

MARY

"What is it, Martha?"

MARTHA

"Come here and help me. Our cousin John should be here any moment and there is much yet to be done. What do you have in hand?"

JOSEPH OF ARIMATHEA

"Mary smiles and holds up a golden silk sash."

MARY

"I made this for him. Do you think he will like it, Lazarus?"

LAZARUS

"Whatever you make for him with your own hands, Mary, Jesus will like."

MARTHA

"And I prepare my best food for him … wash his robe … clean his sandals and all I receive is "Thank you, Martha.""

LAZARUS

"Sisters! Such talk accomplishes nothing. Put your gift away now, Mary, and come help Martha."

JOSEPH OF ARIMATHEA

"Mary begins gathering vegetables from the garden, and Martha carries two full baskets into the house."

MARY

"Lazarus?"

LAZARUS

"Yes, Mary?"

MARY

"Would you tell me more about our cousin John's separation from our Essene community?"

JOSEPH OF ARIMATHEA

Hold it, Lazarus. Before you answer, our friends in the audience may need a little information.

[TO AUDIENCE] The Essenes were a community of ascetics who lived in the Qumran area near the Dead Sea. Little was known about them until 1947 when a Bedouin shepherd boy discovered a cave at the edge of the Dead Sea. In it were broken jars containing scrolls of leather wrapped in linen cloth, inscribed in a strange writing. Some 800 scrolls have been found that tell of this religious order of Essenes – those men and women of the white robes. Both of Jesus' parents were Essenes.

All right, Lazarus. Mary has just asked you why John had separated himself from the Essene Community to which she and your family belong.

LAZARUS

"He hasn't separated himself from our Essene community, Mary. He has become a Nazarite – an Essene who consecrates himself to a total ascetic life."

MARY

"But he is so different from the rest of us Essenes. He raves and preaches as if the world were coming to an end."

LAZARUS

"It's not that the world is coming to an end but to John it's to have a new beginning. He raves and preaches like the Nazarite he is, living a hermit-like life in the wilderness. Our Essene Community here at Bethany is small compared to the Sadducees and Pharisees. John lived in the area of Qumran, around the Dead Sea, where the entire community is Essenes. There are no Sadducees or Pharisees there."

JOSEPH OF ARIMATHEA

Time out, Lazarus! A little more information for our friends in the audience.

[TO AUDIENCE] Probably all of you learned about the Sadducees and Pharisees from Sunday school. You remember how Jesus was always having some problem with them. Obviously, Jesus was not a Sadducee or a Pharisee. The third group of Jews were the Zealots who you probably remember were the hotheads who wanted to destroy Rome's control over Judea. Jesus, of course, was not a Zealot. But one of his twelve disciples was, or at least Judas Iscariot was very friendly with the Zealot's goal of an independent Jewish kingdom. The fourth group in Judea were the Essenes which are not specifically mentioned in your New Testament. Please continue, Lazarus.

LAZARUS

"So, when John came north to preach, he was shocked to discover the rigid practice of the Pharisees, the materialism of the Sadducees, and the war likeness of those Zealots who want nothing but their own kingdom, free of Rome."

MARY

"But he preaches about the coming Kingdom."

LAZARUS

"You are right, Mary, but John's Kingdom is the Kingdom of God. The Zealots wish for a return to an earthly kingdom. They look for a Messiah to overthrow the Roman yoke."

MARY

"And so does John."

LAZARUS

"But not to overthrow Roman rule. The Zealots expect a warrior Messiah. John, like all Essenes, expects a Messiah who is a prophet from God."

MARY

"Is Jesus a disciple of John?"

LAZARUS

"He was when he studied with John before going to Egypt."

MARY

"Lazarus, Martha told me you went with Jesus to Egypt. Is that right?"

LAZARUS

"Yes. He took me with him. Do you remember Joseph of Arimathea who visited us some years ago?"

MARY

"From Arimathea?"

LAZARUS

"Yes. Joseph of Arimathea was one of the first members of the Qumran Essenes to recognize the spiritual qualities of Jesus at a very early age."

"Joseph of Arimathea arranged for Jesus to go to Egypt, which is the source for all Essenes. Jesus asked if I would like to come with him. And I did."

"Well, we've finally finished these chores for Martha. We should go inside and see if she wants us to do anything else."

MARY

"You know she'll have something for us to do, Lazarus. Couldn't we wait a few minutes and you tell me more … before John and Jesus come. After all, shouldn't I know why you and Jesus went to Egypt?"

LAZARUS

"Why not. Come, sit down under the fig tree with me."

JOSEPH OF ARIMATHEA

"Lazarus takes two figs from the tree and gives one to Mary as he sits down beside her."

MARY

"What do you mean when you say Egypt is the source for all Essenes?"

LAZARUS

That is a long story. It began in Egypt nearly two thousand years ago. The great spiritually enlightened Pharaohs of the Amosid Dynasty held private classes in the royal chambers for those few spiritually inclined members of the royal family.

Over the years this White Brotherhood kept alive the worship and knowledge of the one God in opposition to the many gods of Egypt. Towards the end of the Amosid Dynasty, the young Pharaoh called Akhenaton openly declared the spirit of the One God and began destroying the statues of the thousands of Egyptian gods and goddesses.

The priests of Egypt were fearful and enraged, so they decided to kill him. The young Pharaoh then encouraged the Egyptian Prince Moses to leave Egypt and carry the knowledge of One God out of Egypt.

MARY

"You mean our father Moses, who led the Hebrews out of Egypt?"

LAZARUS

"Yes. Moses left the land of Egypt and took with him Egypt's most precious gift – the knowledge of the One God."

MARY

"But Lazarus, our Rabbi has told us many times that the thousands that left Egypt with Moses worshipped idols."

LAZARUS

"But among them were always a small number of spiritual descendants of the White Brotherhood that preserved the knowledge of the One God – just like our large Essene Community near the Dead Sea and small communities of Essenes like our own here at Bethany do now."

MARY

"Why did you and Jesus go to Egypt?"

LAZARUS

"Jesus met and studied under the great prophets in Egypt and experienced the Knowledge of the One God."

MARY

"Did you experience the One God, Lazarus?"

LAZARUS

"Only in my thoughts, Mary, not in my heart. Later, after we returned, Joseph of Arimathea arranged for Jesus to travel to India, but I didn't go with Jesus this time."

MARY

"Why not?"

LAZARUS

"I'm an ordinary man, Mary. Not one of God's prophets."

JOSEPH OF ARIMATHEA

Martha comes out of the house and raises her hands in excitement.

MARTHA

"What are you doing sitting under the tree? Look! He's coming. John will be here in a few moments and I'm not ready! Talk to him while I try to finish everything!"

JOSEPH OF ARIMATHEA

Martha rushes back into the house while Lazarus and Mary get up from under the fig tree and see John approaching.

LAZARUS

"Welcome, John!"

JOHN

"Lazarus, my son, come embrace your dusty old cousin. The last time I was here your mother and father were living. You've increased your lands I see, Lazarus. From the size of your flocks I can see you have become prosperous. And who can this charming girl with sparkling eyes and raven hair be? Not Martha! Is it our little Mary?"

MARY

""Tis I, cousin John."

JOHN

"You're the image of your mother, child. God bless her soul. And Martha? Don't tell me. She's busy getting everything ready."

LAZARUS

"We're to talk with you here while she finishes everything, which may be sometime, John."

JOHN

"Martha never hears the bell because she is always polishing it. And Mary? Mary is always listening for it. Mary, there's a young lamb caught in some twigs down the path. It needs your help."

MARY

"Thank you, cousin John. I'll be back soon, Lazarus."

JOHN

"I have not much time, Lazarus. Soon that old fox King Herod will catch me. But I must meet with Jesus first."

LAZARUS

"Your disciple Andrew told me to expect you and Jesus today."

JOHN

"Andrew is no longer my disciple, Lazarus. He has become a disciple of Jesus. And so has his brother Simon. Since I baptized Jesus, I have become less and he has become more. Herod is not the most alert old fox, for he still seeks me – the lesser – but soon he will seek Jesus. I must warn Jesus of the danger."

LAZARUS

"You baptized Jesus and he is not your disciple?"

JOHN

"Jesus came to me on the banks of the Jordan River and asked to be baptized. I refused. I told him that it was I who should be baptized by him. My mantel should pass to him. But Jesus said, 'You have been and still are my teacher. It is proper for you to baptize me.' And so I began to baptize him. But when my hands moved it was not I moving them. And when I spoke it was not I that formed the words.

"As Jesus arose from the water he lifted his eyes up and I saw a light from heaven upon his face. In my inner ear I heard a voice say, 'This is he in whom I am delighted.'"

LAZARUS

"I'm not sure I understand."

JOHN

"I hadn't baptized Jesus. God had. When we both walked towards the bank, Jesus turned to me and touched me on the shoulder. "Thank you, John," he said. "Your work is done. I am ready now." He walked towards Jerusalem and the crowd followed."

LAZARUS

"And you haven't seen him since?"

JOHN

"I have been told he sought solitude in the wilderness for many days. Some now say he is the Messiah who will deliver us from the Roman yoke. God forbid!"

LAZARUS
"That he might be the Messiah?"

JOHN
"Not the warrior Messiah, Lazarus. But the prophet Messiah, yes. You see, I must be sure. And I must warn him of the danger in going to Jerusalem."

JOSEPH OF ARIMATHEA
Mary hurries to the house carrying a small lamb.

MARY
"He's coming! Jesus is coming. He'll be here in a few moments. I'll tell Martha that he's here."

LAZARUS
"And you can tell her John is here also! You better first ask her if she's ready! Make sure she comes outside. Welcome, Jesus!"

JOSEPH OF ARIMATHEA
Jesus greets and embraces Lazarus and John. Mary and Martha come out of the house.

JESUS
"Mary! Martha! How long has it been? Too long. Come sit down beside me. Here, Mary, on my right."

MARTHA
"The table is not complete, the wine is not yet out…"

JESUS
"Martha! Martha! Be not so busy. Come! Sit down beside me. You can put John, Lazarus and me to work in a few moments, but take this moment and let your thoughts be only with me."

JOSEPH OF ARIMATHEA
They talked of yesterdays, shuddered at John's predictions, and laughed at Jesus' stories.

JESUS

"See, Martha? You can laugh! Now, Lazarus, take your two sisters into the house and John and I shall follow soon. But first he and I must speak a few words."

JOSEPH OF ARIMATHEA

Lazarus, Martha, and Mary enter the house while John and Jesus walk over to the fig tree. Jesus picks a fig from the tree and offers it to John, who shakes his head "No." Jesus then eats it.

JESUS

"Andrew seemed anxious, John. He stressed that it was very important that I meet with you today here at our cousin's home in Bethany."

JOHN

"He's your disciple now.

JESUS

"Yes, he is John."

JOHN

"And so is his brother Simon."

JESUS

"I've given him the name "Peter." Does their discipleship with me bother you, John?"

JOHN

"No, of course not. My work is nearly over. I become less. You, it appears from what I am told, increase."

JESUS

"What are you told, John?"

JOHN

"That you are gathering disciples around you."

JESUS

"Yes, that is true. Others besides Andrew and Peter have joined me in my journey throughout Judea. Even my Essene mentor, Joseph of Arimathea, has become my disciple."

JOHN

"I am told you speak as if from a higher authority to groups that gather around you throughout Judea."

JESUS

"I speak from the same authority as you do, John. You departed from our Essene Community by becoming a Nazarite. I depart from the dead ritual of our Essene Community but not its spiritual message."

JOHN

"I am told you preach the Kingdom of Heaven."

JESUS

"I am your disciple, John. You baptized me. I preach the Kingdom of Heaven, the eternal spiritual abode of God's love."

JOHN

"But you didn't tell your followers to prepare for its coming."

JESUS

"John! John! The Kingdom of Heaven – your message throughout Judea and beyond – is here! Right here. Now. The Kingdom of Heaven is within. Whatever preparation is needed to prepare for its coming is personal preparation. Each individual, even you John, will find the Kingdom – the Kingdom of Heaven we each teach – within himself or herself."

JOHN

"Each individual must redeem himself or herself from sin in preparation of the coming of the Kingdom. That was and is my message."

JESUS

"Without a pure heart no one will enter the Kingdom. Only the pure in heart are able to find the Kingdom of Heaven within themselves. They wait only for their own understanding."

JOHN

"How can I be sure that you are right?"

JESUS

"I came to you as your disciple to be baptized. My baptism was from you, John, but not of you. As we entered the waters of the Jordan, I suddenly felt myself being lifted up and water, not from the Jordan, but from heaven poured over my head and shoulders and body. As I looked up I was filled with light and a spark as bright as the sun came down like a dove upon my brow and I felt embraced in total love. A total love, John, a hundred times, a thousand times more loving than I have ever experienced, even from my earthly father or mother."

JOHN

"I should have known without your telling me. I see now that you are God's child."

JESUS

"We all are, John. But we must discover it by ourselves. It can't be given to us. That's my message, John. The Kingdom I preach is not of this world. It is found within. It must be sought first and then all things shall be given. The psalms tell us to be still and know that God is love."

JOHN

"Herod will not be fooled. Any mention of another Kingdom is a threat to him. After he kills me he will arrest you."

JESUS

"I do not choose my words to avoid Herod. For a while I shall avoid Jerusalem. In a year or two or maybe three, I shall return. That is all the time I need, John. It is all the time granted me."

JOHN

"This is the last time we shall meet in this life, Jesus."

JESUS

"I know. I knew before Andrew gave me your message. There is none born of woman, John, that is greater than you, except that person who discovers the Kingdom of Heaven within."

"Come! Our cousins await us inside. What will unfold soon we will allow them to discover in their own way. We will have a merry feast as this is our last supper together and drink from the fruit of the vine a remembrance of each to the other. You're smiling, John! That is a good sign! Come! Take my arm."

JOSEPH OF ARIMATHEA

A week later, after John is arrested and beheaded, Jesus leaves Judea for Galilee and begins his ministry.

I WILL SEND YOU ELIJAH

A Play about John the Baptizer.

CHARACTERS:
    ANDREW (Narrator), A disciple of John and later of Jesus
    JOHN
    HEROD ANTIPAS ('an tip us), Tetrarch of Galilee
    ELIZABETH, mother of John
    MARTHA, sister of Mary and Lazarus and cousin to John
    MARY MAGDALENE
    SOLOME, daughter of Herodias, wife of Herod Antipas

    PLACE: The dungeon at Machaerus (Ma 'shar us)
    TIME: Shortly before John is beheaded

ANDREW

I am Andrew. I was a disciple of John. John, whom you call the Baptizer. Later, I became a disciple of Jesus. Simon was my brother and I introduced him to Jesus, who gave him the name "Peter." But this story is about John, so I should begin – as they say – in the beginning.

The "beginning" is actually the end. The end of the Old Testament. Malachi is the last book of the Old Testament and ends with these words: "I will send you Elijah." Jesus told his disciples that Elijah had indeed come and they – his disciples – understood that Jesus meant Elijah had returned as John the Baptizer.

John has been imprisoned in the dungeon at Machaerus (Ma 'shar us) by Herod Antipas ('An tip us), the Tetrarch of Galilee. Herod Antipas was one of the many sons of Herod the Great, the King who had all the male babies killed in an effort to rid himself of the coming Messiah. The Herodian kings that ruled in Palestine from 46BC to 100 A. D. had been forcibly converted to Judaism about 125 B. C. Their interest was less in Judaism than in retaining power under the Roman Empire.

Herod Antipas has just entered the dungeon where John is imprisoned. John speaks.

JOHN

"Is that you, you old fox? And you come to me!"

HEROD

"Be still, you old fool. I've come to you out of the goodness of my heart."

JOHN

"Ha!"

HEROD

"Listen to me. I will release you from prison if …"

JOHN

"If! Yes, always 'ifs'!"

HEROD

"We both want the same thing."

JOHN

"I doubt it."

HEROD

"You preach the coming of the Messiah – the leader who will bring back David's kingdom to us. That is what I wish also. A return of David's Kingdom – even greater."

JOHN

"But as your domain under Rome's yoke."

HEROD

"How else, John? Rome rules the world. At present I rule in Galilee, but under Roman power I shall soon rule over Judea and more. Acknowledge that fact, John, that I am the Messiah, and I shall embrace you before all the Jews as our greatest prophet."

JOHN

"You would embrace me? You've imprisoned me."

HEROD

"It was not my wish to imprison you, but Herodias, my wife's wish."

JOHN

"That unprincipled, designing woman is the wife of your brother Philip! She bewitched you into marrying her, for you promise greater riches and fame than that aged Philip. She is a fornicator and I denounce her again."

HEROD

"Yes, yes, yes. That is why you are here! It is bad enough that you agitated the people about some approaching kingdom, but you dared question Herodias's morality! She was furious with your accusations against her.

I had to silence you, John. I can soothe Herodias's bitterness with another diamond necklace, if you but declare for me, John. Then you shall go free. We both want the return of David's kingdom."

JOHN

"You want the return of David's kingdom for power and greed. Too many expect a Messiah with a sword. You are not the Messiah, Herod. But the true Messiah has come! He has come in love and sacrifice and brings the good news of God's kingdom."

ANDREW

Herod grabs John's throat and yells.

HEROD

"Where? Where is he? Tell me, or I'll have you…"

JOHN

"Killed? Herod, Herod! You dally on the outside of God's great plans. I will have nothing more to do with you. Be gone, you simple fool!"

HEROD

"You call me fool? You, who never has sat with a woman, felt her warm caress, or tasted the ruby lips of a young virgin, you are a fool! You can rot here."

ANDREW

Herod leaves the dungeon and John reflects on Herod's last words and thinks of the women in his life. The image of his mother, Elizabeth, comes into his view. She speaks.

ELIZABETH

"John! Oh, John, my dear child!"

JOHN

"My sweet mother! How I have hungered for your tender caress."

ANDREW

Elizabeth takes the hem of her shawl and wipes John's brow.

ELIZABETH

"This is not what we intended for you. Your father and I dedicated you to God."

JOHN

"My life is dedicated to God, mother, and that life is near its end, its mission is nearly completed and God's plan for me nearly fulfilled."

ELIZABETH

"But this…"

JOHN

"This dungeon contains only my body, mother, it can never contain my spirit. My being here keeps that fox Herod from God's chosen Messiah, at least for a while, until his mission is accomplished."

ELIZABETH

"The Messiah? Who, John?"

JOHN

"Our cousin Jesus. Last month he came to me to be baptized. I baptized him with water but suddenly I became overwhelmed by a great feeling of love that descended upon Jesus and baptized him with God's spirit."

ELIZABETH

"Jesus? My dear cousin Mary's first child? Now I begin to understand, John."

JOHN

"Yes, Mother, and so do I. What I preached in the wilderness he now declares in the towns. My task, the task for which you and my father raised me, is completed. I shall soon join both of you."

ANDREW

Elizabeth bends down and kisses John, strokes his head and passes from his vision. A soft voice whispers, "John?" It is the voice of Martha, the sister of Mary and Lazarus.

JOHN

"I know that voice. Is it you, cousin Martha?"

MARTHA

"Yes, John, it is your little cousin Martha. But this is no place for you. You are God's voice in the wilderness and do not deserve such treatment. Herod is a tyrant!"

JOHN

"Be not so concerned, Martha. We all have our roles to play in life. Herod, a weak, but peaceful man, chose his role long ago. And so did I. Only mine was and is by God's will. But where are Mary and Lazarus?"

MARTHA

"They minister to Jesus now."

JOHN

"But you were always the practical one. You should be with him now."

MARTHA

"But I am, John, by being here…for you. You have been the tree and now Jesus is the blossom. The tree may be cut down even while the blossom unfolds."

JOHN

"Oh, Martha! I fear blossoms bloom for too short a time."

MARTHA

"Perhaps. But seeds arise within the dying blossom."

JOHN

"His time will be short."

MARTHA

"Yes, John. But long enough. Herod's concern with you, assures Jesus of that time. Your sacrifice brings into being the good news you have preached."

ANDREW

John lifts his hand as a blessing for Martha and, smiling, nods his head. Martha fades into the shadows and John leans back against the wet stone wall and sighs.

A pale light in the corner of the dungeon slowly brightens and the figure of Mary Magdalene appears. She speaks.

MARY

"John? It is I. Mary Magdalene."

JOHN

"Mary? Mary Magdalene! Have you come from him?"

MARY

"Yes. But I have come to you. Jesus is fully aware of where and why you are here. He gives you his blessing, John. He begins to live your good news about the kingdom of heaven that it is within each of us – now – and not outside of our own time and our own space."

JOHN

"Why, Mary Magdalene, you sound like a disciple."

MARY

"I am, John. He calls me his "Sister of the Spirit." In my fallen state, Jesus not only picked me up but took me under his spiritual protection. The crowds follow him by the hundreds, John. I and a few other of his female followers provide for his simple needs. He has gathered a band of disciples that accompany him on his journey around Galilee. Some once followed you."

JOHN

"That is as it should be. My light fades; his begins to glow. Jesus will need their support. But I am concerned for I hear that he does not baptize."

MARY

"Not with water, John. But with God's spirit. The kingdom that you preached and said was near, Jesus declares is <u>here</u> – within. You have accomplished your task."

ANDREW

Mary Magdalene kisses John's brow, turns about and leaves John's vision. John lifts his head and speaks to God.

JOHN

"You do work in mysterious ways, Lord. My own cousin. Just a few months younger than I. For years I preached his coming, and didn't know it was he, my own cousin Jesus. You could have made it simpler. I had heard much about him, about his travels to far eastern lands. I was pleased when he joined with my disciples to hear me bring the good news of the kingdom. He always had that assurance, that spiritual quality that I seemed to lack. When he came to me last month and said he wished to receive baptism from me, I suddenly realized that he was the one! It was like a mist vaporizing before me, and I saw Jesus not as my cousin, not as my disciple, but as my master.

I am like Elijah and pass my mantle on to Elisha."

ANDREW

John is wiser than he thinks. Indeed, <u>he</u> had been Elijah. Elijah's young disciple Elisha asked if he could become Elijah's successor. Elijah put the matter in God's hands, saying Elisha would get his request only if God allowed him to see what was about to happen. Suddenly a chariot of fire appeared, drawn by horses of fire. It drove between them, separating them, and Elijah was carried by a whirlwind into heaven. Elisha saw it. Elisha then picked up Elijah's cloak and when he came to the river, it parted when touched by the rolled-up cloak.

Elisha knew then that God had granted his request.

When John was asked if he was Elijah, he said no. God, not in mystification, but in His compassion, allowed John to forget his previous role as Elijah -- such memory would only have been a further burden to him in his role as John.

John has one more vision. In the distance he hears music and laughter, the voices of young boys and girls. A cloud emerges in the corner of his dungeon and begins to form into the body of a young girl poised to dance. Startled, John stands up and watches the sprite figure bow with open arms. John speaks.

                                    JOHN

"Solome!"

                                    SOLOME

"You remember me!"

                                    JOHN

"How could I forget. There you were, a small child lost in the desert."

                                    SOLOME

"You do remember! My sobbing and crying stopped when your strong arms picked me up and your gentle eyes assured me I was now safe. You asked me who I was and then took me to my mother."

                                    JOHN

"She was not then Philip's wife."

                                    SOLOME

"She liked you."

                                    JOHN

"Ah!"

                                    SOLOME

"You spurned her, John. And now you have humiliated her as Herod's wife. She is very strong willed and does not forget."

JOHN

"And you, child, is she good to you?"

SOLOME

"She gives me everything I want. I would do anything for her. That is why I have come to you now, John. You were so kind and gentle to me, saving me from a cold and lonely death. Make your peace with Herodias, with my mother. I don't want you, my personal savior, to be imprisoned. Please, John. Next to my mother, I would do anything to help you.

Tonight, I dance before Herod. That old fool looks upon me with more than fatherly eyes, John. I shall please him and he will grant me whatever I wish."

JOHN

"Child, Child, beware of that lecherous old fool and do not let your sweet innocence be influenced by the foul spirit of your mother. You will please me most by gaining righteousness for your own soul. Beware of Herod and listen not to the evil from your mother. Be careful of the role you choose."

SOLOME

"I am glad that I can dance. If that is my role, so much the better. What ever my role is, it will surely be insignificant. All these other matters are too confusing for me. Gentle John, You saved my life. For that I am most gracious. I shall think of you being in better circumstances when I dance tonight."

ANDREW

Solome prances toward John, takes his two big hands with her small ones, and kisses them. She dances into the cloud and the sudden darkness causes John to slump to the floor.

I, Andrew, now find myself standing in John's cell with the pale light of a full moon shining on him. I speak. "Master?"

JOHN

"Who's there? Who calls me Master?"

ANDREW

"Andrew. Your disciple."

JOHN

"Why, Andrew! How good it is to see you. But you <u>were</u> my disciple. You follow Jesus now. He is your Master. You are his disciple."

ANDREW

"That is right, John, but…"

JOHN

"You need not explain, Andrew. You and the other of my disciples that became his did so with my encouragement and approval. It is as it should be."

ANDREW

"Your imprisonment gives Jesus the time he needs."

JOHN

"It keeps Herod busy. Yes, I know that."

ANDREW

"Your death will also provide Jesus more time."

JOHN

"Of course. I did not spend my entire life as a herald of God's message without knowing the final act of the drama, Andrew. I am not this body, Andrew. I am my soul, and it is eternal. The only true death is death itself. A moment on the wheel of life and another end becomes a new beginning.

Tell Jesus that his suffering in his final hours will be longer than mine. Tell him he shall not be able to feel my presence in his last moments because of the agony his body will experience. My last moments in this body will be but the flick of an eyelash. But through all his days, except in his final moments in his body, I shall be by his side. Tell him that, Andrew. God will be the cause that sustains him but I will be the means."

ANDREW

John blessed me and then lay down on his straw mat.

That night, Solome danced before Herod and that night John's head was severed from his body and given on a charger to Herodias by Solome.

On the ninth hour when Jesus was crucified he cried with a loud voice, "Eli, Eli, lama sabach-tha-ni?" Some thought he said "My God, my God, why hast thou forsaken me?" But some bystanders said, "This man is calling Elijah."

* * *

PILATE

A play about the trial of Jesus

CHARACTERS:
    PONTIUS PILATE, Governor of Judea
    CAIAPHAS, High priest
    JESUS
    MARCUS QUINTUS, Senior Centurion, aide to Pilate
    NARRATOR: Hipparchus, a Greek slave from Athens

PLACE: The Praetorium, the residence of the Governor of Judea
TIME: 30 A.D.

NARRATOR

I am Hipparchus, a Greek slave in the service of Pontius Pilate, the Governor of Judea.

There are a few names, perhaps, we should identify, to assure you of enjoying our play.
    Barabbas was a Jewish insurrectionist who was imprisoned at the time of Jesus' trial.
    Herod is the ruler of Galilee. He was the son of Herod the Great, the ruler who attempted to kill the baby Jesus.
    Caiaphas is the Jewish high priest.
    Marcus Quintus is a senior centurion and aide to Pilate.

The Mysteries, which Pilate refers to, are the secret rites of esoteric philosophies of that time in which priests, initiates, and new disciples enacted allegorical scenes from the lives of gods and goddesses. Their secret meaning was explained to new members upon initiation. There were the Greek mysteries and the Egyptian mysteries, but most Roman soldiers were initiates of the mysteries of Mithras.

Our play opens in the praetorian, the residence of the Roman governors of Judea, Pontius Pilate, a cunning, vicious, ambitious Roman, who has been governor for three years. Caiaphas, the high priest, speaks to Pilate and nods to Marcus Quintus, the senior Centurion who stands next to Pilate.

SCENE 1

CAIAPHAS

"Most gracious governor, on the behalf of the Jewish Sanhedrin, I have come to you for help to prevent trouble."

PILATE

"That is the only thing you Jews do, is make trouble. What now?"

CAIAPHAS

"I humbly beg your indulgence. Since Rome appointed me high priest, I have prevented even the smallest disturbance, let alone rebellion by those Jews who do not appreciate the great peace which Roman has brought to Judea."

PILATE

"I am immune to your lofty words, Caiaphas. What is it you want? Contents, Caiaphas."

CAIAPHAS

"That Nazarene instigator, Jesus, is expected to come into Jerusalem during our Passover festival."

PILATE

"I understand your concern, Caiaphas. It is reported to me that he attracts thousands in the desert. It doesn't help your business."

CAIAPHAS

"The governor jests. If it is a business, it is the business of our God. There is always much turmoil during the Passover festival and this Jesus and his followers will only add to it. We ask you to arrest him when he comes to Jerusalem."

PILATE

"The rebel Barabbas is in prison, and I am grateful to you for your help, Caiaphas. But this Jesus, I am told, has no soldiers, carries no weapons, does not incite the crowds to rebellion against Rome."

CAIAPHAS
"He is an agitator, my lord, and challenges the teachings of our holy Torah."

PILATE
"Rome gives equal protection to all religions, all the mysteries, all prophets, as long as they obey Roman law and give homage to Caesar. I fear, my dear Caiaphas, that you have a problem of religious ideas, and that is not a concern for Rome. No matter how disrupting those ideas, that is your jurisdiction, but the slightest act of trouble will be immediately put down. There will be no trouble in Judea while I am governor."

CAIAPHAS
"My lord, there is dissension within the Sanhedrin and his presence in Jerusalem will only further it."

PILATE
"My dear, Caiaphas, use the power and authority you have to contain any dissension that might occur among you, if this Jesus fellow should come to Jerusalem."

CAIAPHAS
"As you say, my Lord. I take leave of you. Shalom!"

PILATE
"Marcus, what do you know of this Jesus? What I have heard of his preaching sounds as if it is one of the mysteries. Aren't most of our legionnaires followers of Mithras?"

MARCUS QUINTUS
"Yes, my lord."

PILATE
"And you?"

MARCUS QUINTUS
"Yes, my lord, I am a follower of Mithras. Mithras devoted his life on earth to the service of mankind and we believe he ascended to heaven and continues to help us."

PILATE

"You attended a Mithras celebration with a large number of our legionnaires this past December. Isn't that true?"

MARCUS QUINTUS

"On the 25th of December, my lord. It is Mithras's birthday. It's a simple celebration of bread and wine."

PILATE

"That's good for our legionnaires. This Jesus might even be good for the Jews!
My wife told me one of her Jewish maids has seen Jesus heal her sick mother of a skin disease."

MARCUS QUINTUS

"Our centurion Gallus told me that when his servant was ill, he sent a messenger to this Jesus and asked him to heal his servant. Apparently this Jesus was impressed with the message. Gallus said that he, a centurion, was a man of authority that said this shall be done and it was, and he knew that Jesus was such a man of authority and had only to say his servant was healed and it would be. His servant was healed instantly."

PILATE

"Marcus, keep your eyes and ears alert should this Jesus come to Jerusalem. When I left Rome, the emperor told me he wanted but two things from me: taxes and order."

SCENE 2

NARRATOR

A week has passed. Jesus did come to Jerusalem and was hailed by the Jews as their king. He entered the temple and with a rope in his hand drove the money changers out. Caiaphas speaks to the members of the Sanhedrin.

CAIAPHAS

"This attack by Jesus in the temple is directed at us, because we wish to keep the peace through the collaboration of Rome and our Temple functions. If more and more people come to believe in him and his miracles, he will constitute a threat that the Romans might use as a reason to destroy the Temple and the Nation. In the turmoil of the Passover, the fervor over Jesus could become a rebellion. Jesus must be arrested before the Passover festival. One of his followers has informed me where he can be found this evening. I have ordered our temple guards to arrest Jesus. It is better for one to die than many."

SCENE 3

NARRATOR

It is the same evening. Since it is nearly the Passover, Caiaphas cannot enter the Praetorian because he would become polluted. Pilate, therefore, steps on the grounds to meet Caiaphas. Caiaphas speaks.

CAIAPHAS

"My thanks to my lord governor for seeing me outside of his praetorian."

PILATE

'To the point Caiaphas. What is it you want?"

CAIAPHAS

"Jesus has not only come to Jerusalem but has disrupted the normal business of the temple."

PILATE

"This was reported to me. He knocked over the tables of your money changers and drove them out with a rope. Is that correct?"

CAIAPHAS

"Yes, my lord governor. These rebellious Galileans have desecrated the temple and instigated trouble among the people. We have arrested him this night and brought him to you for judgment."

PILATE

"You've arrested him? (Surprised) You said he is a Galilean?"

CAIAPHAS

"Yes, my lord governor. His immediate followers are uncouth Galileans except for one Jew, the one called Judas, who informed us where to find him."

PILATE

"Take him to Herod! He's governor of Galilee. If he's from Galilee he comes under Herod's jurisdiction. Now go! I wish to hear no more about it."

CAIAPHAS
"I shall do as you bid."

PILATE
"Well, Marcus, we'll let that old fox Herod handle this. I've never liked him. He would like to increase his authority at my expense. He's as crafty as his father was."

MARCUS QUINTUS
"Craftier, I have been told, my lord."

SCENE 4

NARRATOR

Jesus is taken to Herod, who is at his palace in Jerusalem. Herod mocks Jesus but concludes that he is an innocent man of no harm. He tells Caiaphas to take Jesus back to Pilate with his best wishes.

It is the next morning and Caiaphas speaks to Pilate.

CAIAPHAS

"Herod sends his good wishes to the governor of Judea. He bows to your judgment and returns the prisoner Jesus to you."

PILATE

"Do you hear that, Marcus? Perhaps Herod isn't as bad as I thought. We might even become friends."

CAIAPHAS

"Witnesses have testified that Jesus said he would be able to destroy the temple of God and re build it in three days."

PILATE

"A serious accusation but that is your concern not Rome's."

CAIAPHAS

"He says he is our king."

PILATE

"Your king?"

CAIAPHAS

"Yes, my lord, but we have no king but Caesar."

PILATE

"Rome makes kings, Caiaphas."

CAIAPHAS

"Then Rome must crucify Jesus. We cannot."

PILATE

"I determine who is crucified, Caiaphas.
Marcus, bring me the prisoner."

NARRATOR

Jesus is brought before Pilate. He has been dressed in a purple robe and a makeshift crown made by Herod as a mocking jest for Pilate's pleasure.

PILATE

"Can this creature be a king?

Are you a king?" (Mockingly, to Jesus.)

JESUS

"Did they tell you to ask this?"

NARRATOR

A guard slaps Jesus' face. Pilate motions with his hand for the guard to pull back.

PILATE

"It is a simple question. If you are a king, where is your kingdom?"

JESUS

"My kingdom is not of this world."

PILATE

"But you wish to die for this kingdom?"

JESUS

"I do not seek death, but I follow a path of truth which may lead to death."

PILATE

"Truth! Ah, yes, truth.
I see no danger in this innocent fool. Caiaphas. He may be a threat to you Jews but not to Rome."

CAIAPHAS

"The mob, those who would follow Barabbas, see him as their king. My lord governor, if Jesus is not put to death and is set free, he will become the symbol for rebellion against Rome."

PILATE

"Could this happen, Marcus?"

MARCUS QUINTUS

"The actions of Jesus and his followers are no threat to Rome, my lord, but his words have been interpreted by the Jews as a promise to restore the Kingdom of Israel. If he lives, he will become the fire that ignites the brush."

PILATE

"That can never be! These fanatical Jews think they are a special people. Any uprising in Judea and Caesar will have my head! Better to send an innocent man to his death than to displease Caesar.

I declare Jesus a rebel against Rome!

Arrange for his crucifixion, Marcus.

Caiaphas, you and your Sanhedrin are indebted to me."

CAIAPHAS

"I and they are pleased that this will soon end through your actions. We are your lordship's servants."

SCENE 5

NARRATOR

Jesus is crucified between two criminals. That evening Marcus Quintus reports to Pilate.

MARCUS QUINTUS

"My lord, the crucifixion has been carried out. Jesus died within a short time and his legs did not have to be broken. Some of his followers had gathered around him, but there has been no trouble."

PILATE

"Well done, Marcus."

MARCUS QUINTUS

"I put Gallus in charge of the crucifixion, my lord."

PILATE

"The centurion who asked that his servant be healed?"

MARCUS QUINTUS

"Yes, my lord. He was not pleased by the order, but he is a capable centurion who does his duty."

PILATE

"I like the irony, Marcus. Gallus crucifies the man who helped him."

MARCUS QUINTUS

"Gallus said the only help he could provide the prisoner was to take someone from the crowd to carry the cross for Jesus. He said that when the man took the cross from him, Jesus looked into his eyes and that caused Gallus to feel a tremendous sense of peace come over him."

PILATE

'Your centurion Gallus has a sensitive streak. That bears watching, Marcus. But, come with me. This has been one of those trying days that will soon be forgotten."

NARRATOR

Pilate was later exiled to France, where he committed suicide.

In 1990 an ornate, first century family burial box was found beneath Jerusalem which contained bones of a man of about sixty, who scholars say was likely the high priest himself.

A decade after his death, Caiaphas's fears were realized when the Jewish Revolt ended with Rome destroying the last Jewish Temple.

I, the slave Hipparchus, was bought by Marcus Quintus when he was granted land in southern Gaul (which you call France) After twenty years of service in the Roman army, he set me free, but I continued to serve him.

We both became disciples of Jesus.

THE FIRST EASTER

A play about the crucifixion and resurrection of Jesus.

CHARACTERS:
    CLEOPAS: Narrator of the story as well as being a follower of Jesus
    JOANNA: The sister of Cleopas and friend of Mary Magdalene
    CAIAPHAS: High Priest
    SIMEON: Servant to Caiaphas
    JESUS
    MARY MAGDALENE

    PLACE: Present day Israel
    TIMES: 30 A.D.

SCENE 1

CLEOPAS

My name is Cleopas [KLEE o pus]. I am a follower of Jesus along with my sister, Joanna, who is one of the women who nurtured Jesus and his immediate disciples in their journeys throughout Judea and Galilee. She accompanied Mary Magdalene to the tomb where Jesus' body was temporarily placed. But more of that later.

The time is early April in the year 783, according to the Roman calendar, but the year 30 by your present calendar. It is the time of the Jewish Passover, but with time, it will become the Christian celebration of the resurrection of Jesus. Interestingly, it will be called, "Easter," which is a Teutonic name for the Goddess of Spring as well as their celebration of Spring.

Our play, entitled "The First Easter," takes place on the Sunday after Jesus' crucifixion two days before -- on Friday. The first scene occurs early that morning in the home of the chief priest, Caiaphas [KYE uh fuss], who became extremely distraught upon being informed that the body of Jesus has disappeared from the tomb. The second scene finds Mary Magdalene and Joanna, who are both followers of Jesus, going to the tomb just before dawn to anoint his body. The Third scene is about the mysterious and wonderful stranger that my sister and I encountered that afternoon when we walked to Emmaus [em MAY us].

Now for our first scene, in the early hours of Sunday morning. Simeon [SIM ee uhn], the personal servant of the Chief Priest Caiaphas, has his master awakened. Caiaphas speaks:

CAIAPHAS

"What is it, Simeon? It's many hours until dawn. This has been a strenuous week for me, and it has taken all my strength finally to have gotten rid of that trouble maker. You're shaking, Simeon. Out with it. Speak, man!"

SIMEON

"He's.. he's … gone!"

CAIAPHAS

"What? Who's gone?"

SIMEON

"Je … je … sus, the trouble maker."

CAIAPHAS

"Gone! What do you mean, gone?"

SIMEON

"Hi .. hi.. his…"

CAIAPHAS

"Calm yourself, Simeon. Sit down. Now take a deep breath and then start at the beginning."

SIMEON

"Thank you, my lord. I am now composed." [Taking several deep breaths] "The trouble maker, Jesus. His body has disappeared from the tomb."

CAIAPHAS

"Disappeared! How is that possible? Surely you are mistaken, Simeon. That is the very reason I went to the Governor: to provide Roman soldiers to guard the tomb to prevent Jesus' disciples from stealing his body. You, yourself, Simeon, reported to me that he kept saying he would rise again in three days. Pilate provided soldiers. What about the soldiers, Simeon?"

SIMEON

"The captain of our temple guard informs me that the Roman soldiers had fallen asleep or perhaps been drugged."

CAIAPHAS

"Impossible! Roman soldiers do not fall asleep or become drugged. Pilate will have them crucified! What has happened to them?"

SIMEON

"They are outside, my lord. The two men have come to us. They told me that an earthquake rolled the stone away from the tomb and they feared their god was punishing them. They believe Jesus is a miracle worker even if dead."

CAIAPHAS

"These superstitious gentiles! His disciples have stolen his body! By Tuesday they will proclaim that 'he has risen from the dead.' Will we never be able to rid ourselves of this man and his simple followers?

What should I do with the two soldiers?"

CAIAPHAS

"Listen carefully, Simeon. Pay them, and not a small sum. Tell them to report to their Centurion that Jesus' disciples came by night and stole his body while they were sleeping. Assure them, that if Pilate the governor, hears of it, we will appeal to him and declare that they are blameless. And, Simeon, call the members of the Sanhedrin to meet just after dawn today. Go!"

SIMEON

"My lord, do you believe his disciples have taken his body?"

CAIAPHAS

"Of course! Now, Leave, Simeon."

SCENE 2

CLEOPAS

It is a few hours later, just before dawn on Sunday morning. Mary Magdalene and Joanna, two of Jesus' devoted women followers, walk to the tomb where his body now rests. Joanna carries jars of spices and perfumes, with which she and Mary Magdalene intend to anoint Jesus' body. Mary Magdalene speaks:

MARY MAGDALENE

"There, Joanna. Just ahead. There, the tomb is not many steps ahead. Let me help you carry the spices."

JOANNA

"It is no trouble, Mary. They're not heavy. Oh, Mary! How sad I am. To anoint our Lord! What will become of us?"

MARY MAGDALENE

"Everything will be all right, Joanna. The Teacher looks over us and his followers even in death. Be of good heart. In a few moments we will be with him. We should be so pleased that Joseph of Arimathea asked us to anoint his body."

JOANNA

"These jars of spices that Nicodemus gave us to anoint the body of Jesus are the most fragrant mixture of myrrh and aloes I have come across, Mary. They must be very expensive. I did not know that he as well as Joseph were followers of our Lord."

MARY MAGDALENE

"Both Nicodemus and Joseph are members of the Sanhedrin, as you know, and must keep secret that they are followers of our Lord."

JOANNA

"Didn't Joseph beseech Pilate that he might take away the body of Jesus?"

MARY MAGDALENE

"Yes. He knows the governor personally. Pilate wished to please him, and allowed him to take the body. The Sanhedrin may assume that Joseph did this in order not to have Jesus' body taken down later during the Sabbath."

JOANNA

"Well, isn't that the reason Jesus was taken down from the cross much earlier than is normal?"

MARY MAGDALENE

"You were there, Joanna. You saw how soon our Lord gave up the ghost after his crucifixion."

JOANNA

"How can I ever forget, Mary? God did not wish him to suffer more."

MARY MAGDALENE

"I am told that the Roman soldiers break the legs of the crucified to hasten death, and Joseph wished to take Jesus' body down from the cross before they might break his legs, even though he was dead."

JOANNA

"How horrible! To crucify and then have one's legs broken. How cruel these Romans are!"

MARY MAGDALENE

"Cruel, yes, Joanna, but not in this act."

JOANNA

"What do you mean?"

MARY MAGDALENE

"A crucified person can no longer support his body with his legs broken. This makes breathing very difficult and soon brings on death. You see, it's really done as an act of mercy."

JOANNA

"I don't want to hear any more, Mary! It's too hard to bear. Our poor, dear precious Lord."

MARY MAGDALENE

"We are nearly there, Joanna. One of the guards will be able to roll the stone from the entrance, I am sure.

See, Joanna, the first rays of the sun light our path. Look! There is the tomb."

JOANNA

"Where are the guards?"

MARY MAGDALENE

"That's strange. There are no guards?"

JOANNA

"I thought Roman soldiers were ordered to guard the entrance to the tomb?"

MARY MAGDALENE

"They were. Joseph arranged that with Pilate. See? On the ground, a Roman spear. Someone of authority was here. Whoever was here, left in a hurry. It is very strange, Joanna."

JOANNA

"Mary! The door to the tomb!"

MARY MAGDALENE

"It's been rolled back. The entrance is open. Where are you going, Joanna?"

JOANNA

"Mary! It's empty! The tomb is empty. I'm frightened. I'm going back to the disciples. Come with me. Something is not right. I'm scared. Let us go."

MARY MAGDALENE

"I shall stay here, Joanna. Tell the disciples what we have found here. God go with you."

CLEOPAS

Joanna runs away and Mary kneels down in prayer.

The sun rises and the dawn mist fades and Mary continues to pray on her knees. The sound of someone approaching from the path disturbs her meditation and she sees Peter hurry on the path. She speaks to him, but he says nothing. He walks quickly into the tomb. He sees the burial cloth and notices that the cloth that had covered Jesus' head is not with the burial cloth, but rolled up in a separate place. A few moments later he leaves the tomb and with a bewildered look, walks past Mary, back to the path without saying a word.

Mary continues to pray until some disturbance causes her to look at the tomb entrance. She opens her eyes and sees a figure standing by the side of the open tomb. She speaks:

MARY MAGDALENE

"Are you the gardener? Oh, kind sir, please tell me where you have lain the body of our Lord? Please tell me where have you placed him?"

CLEOPAS

The figure is not the gardener. It is Jesus. He speaks softly:

JESUS

"Mary!"

MARY MAGDALENE

"Teacher? Oh, teacher!"

CLEOPAS

Mary rushes to the feet of Jesus.

JESUS

"Do not touch me now, Mary. I am not yet complete."

MARY MAGDALENE

"My Lord, you are not dead!"

JESUS

"Not now, Mary. My body died. Have I not said many times to you and our brothers and sisters, and even to the crowds, that I would arise in three days? Tomorrow will be three days, Mary. I am not yet ready."

MARY MAGDALENE

"Oh, Lord, how wonderful to have you back! The disciples have scattered and will be thrilled to know you are again with us."

JESUS

"Dear Mary. My blessed Mary. I would that I might gently caress your cheek, but I cannot at this time. Tomorrow I shall be in Galilee and then I will dry your loving tears and bless that angelic head that smiles at me. Go to Galilee and tell the disciples what you have seen, what you have heard. Go. Things will come to pass tomorrow. That will be the third day."

(PAUSE)

CLEOPAS (as narrator)

Jesus lifts his right hand in the gesture of a blessing and suddenly is no longer there in any physical form. Mary slowly rises, turns to the sunlit path and begins her journey to Galilee, smiling, crying, oh, so utterly happy!

SCENE 3

CLEOPAS (as narrator)

The third and last scene of our play finds me and my sister Joanna walking to Emmaus, which is an hour from Jerusalem. It is the same day around noon. I am speaking to Joanna when a stranger, whom we do not discover until later is Jesus, suddenly speaks to us.

CLEOPAS

"Yes, Joanna, you are right. Joseph of Arimathea is a good and righteous man. He follows the Teacher's message and seeks the Kingdom of God."

JOANNA

"It was he who took our Lord down from the cross."

CLEOPAS

"You are right. It was he who wrapped the body of our Teacher in fine linen and laid it in that tomb you said you and Mary Magdalene visited. I was told that when Joseph obtained permission to take down our Teacher's body from the cross, he and other brothers needed a place to put the body until they could arrange for a more proper tomb; so Joseph took the body to the very tomb he had recently had hewn out for his own future tomb."

STRANGER (JESUS)

"What are these words that you are discussing with each other, as you walk?"

CLEOPAS

"Are you alone a stranger from Jerusalem, that you do not know what happened in these last several days?"

JESUS

"Tell me about these things that have happened."

JOANNA

"We speak of Jesus of Nazareth, who entered Jerusalem only last week to the great jubilation of the people. He was their hope to save Israel and whom some even declared to be "King of the Jews." He was a prophet, mighty in word and deed before God and before the people."

JESUS

"Is he no longer here?"

CLEOPAS

"Then you have not heard. He was crucified by the Romans two days ago. He was taken into the Preatorium and the whole body of onlookers gathered about him. The Roman soldiers removed his clothes and put on him a scarlet robe, mocking him, saying, "Hail, King of the Jews!"

JOANNA

"They took him to Golgotha where he was crucified between two thieves. I was there with my friend Mary. We saw how our innocent, righteous teacher suffered under the horrible treatment of the Roman soldiers."

JESUS

"Perhaps he did not trust in God to save himself."

CLEOPAS

"My dear sir, he had no need to be saved. He could have called forth ten legion of angels; but you know what he prayed? "Father, forgive them, for they know not what they do."

JESUS

"So yet another prophet of God has been killed."

JOANNA

"But not gone. He often mentioned to us, those who are his followers, 'I shall arise in three days.' When the scribes and Pharisees demanded that he show them some sign of authority, he replied, 'No sign shall be given to this evil generation, unless it be the sign of Jonah.'"

JESUS

"The sign of Jonah? That is a strange reply."

CLEOPAS

"Not at all, sir. He meant that the three days Jonah spent in the stomach of a whale were like the three days he would be gone before being resurrected from the dead."

JESUS

"I am no stranger to the story of Jonah, but being resurrected from the dead, and in three days – my friends, this is difficult to believe."

JOANNA

"Sir, my friend Mary and I were at the tomb where they had placed his body after his crucifixion. We were surprised to find the huge stone that hoarded the entrance to the tomb had been rolled away. I looked into the tomb. It was empty."

JESUS

"An empty tomb is hardly evidence of being resurrected from the dead, my child."

CLEOPAS

"Tell him what Mary told you, Joanna."

JOANNA

"I left after seeing the empty tomb but my friend Mary remained. She told me that later a man stood in front of the tomb whom she thought at first was the gardener. But it was Jesus, resurrected from the dead. Overjoyed, she touched his feet in homage, but he told her not to touch him at that moment. He said that he was not yet 'complete.' He told her to go to our community and tell them that she had seen Jesus and spoken with him, and that on the third day, which is tomorrow, he would appear before them in Galilee."

CLEOPAS

"That is where we are headed, sir."

JESUS

"And so am I."

CLEOPAS

"The day is spent and it is near dark. Emmaus is only a few steps ahead. Stay there with us this evening. Look! There is an inn where we can obtain a meal and lodgings."

JOANNA

"Please join us. This should be a quiet place. In the corner is a table with three chairs. May we not sit there?"

JESUS

"Thank you. I shall sit here, where I might see the both of you. Thank you, innkeeper. Allow me to break this bread which the innkeeper has placed before us and bless it. Please close your eyes in prayer and open your hearts. (PRAYS) Father, Thank You for the gift of life. Bless this bread that becomes a sacred sign of Your presence. You may open your eyes now, my children…"

CLEOPAS

"Master!"

###

APPENDIX

SEVEN REFERENCES TO WHY JESUS CAME:

1) He said to them, Let us walk to the neighboring towns, so that I may preach there also, FOR I CAME FOR THIS. **Mark 1:38**

2) I must preach the Kingdom of God to other cities also, BECAUSE I WAS SENT FOR THIS. **Luke 4:43**

3) Do not suppose that I HAVE COME to bring peace on earth: I have not come to bring peace but a sword. **Matthew 10:34**

4) I HAVE COME to set a man against his father and a daughter against her mother. **Matthew 10:35**

5) I HAVE COME that they might have life, and have it more abundantly. **John 10:10**

6) The Son 0f Man HAS COME to seek and to save what was lost. **Luke 19:10**

7) I have come to save the world, not judge it. **John 12:47**

REFERENCES TO THE KINGDOM OF HEAVEN:

1) Repent ye, for the Kingdom of Heaven is at hand. **Matthew 3:2**

2) 1 (Jesus:) Except a man be born again, he cannot see the Kingdom of God.

3) 2 (Jesus:) Except a man be born of water and of Spirit he cannot enter into the Kingdom of God. **John 3:3**

4) Jesus came into Galilee, preaching the Gospel of the Kingdom of God. **Mark 1:14**

5-6) from that time Jesus began to preach and to say, Repent; for the Kingdom of Heaven is at hand. **Matthew 4:17**

7)Now after that John was put in prison, Jesus came to Galilee preaching the gospel of the Kingdom of God. **Mark 1:14**

8) And saying, The time is fulfilled, and the Kingdom of God is at hand; repent and believe the gospel. **Mark 1:15**

9) From that time~ [Leaving Nazareth and dwelling in Capernaum] Jesus began to preach and to say, Repent, for the kingdom of Heaven is coming near. **Matthew 4:17**

10-11) Jesus traveled throughout Galilee, teaching in their synagogues and preach the gospel of the kingdom, and healing all manner of sickness and disease among the people. **Matthew 4:23**

12) These twelve Jesus sent out, and charged them and said, Keep away from pagan practices, and do not enter a Samaritan city; but above all go to the sheep which are lost from the house of Israel. Preach and say that the Kingdom of Heaven is near. **Matthew 10: 5,6,7**

SERMON ON THE MOUNT
Matthew 5,6,7

13-14) BLESSED are those unattached to earthly possessions, for theirs is the Kingdom of Heaven. Blessed are you poor, for the Kingdom of Heaven is yours. **Luke 6: 21**

15) BLESSED are they who are steadfast in righteousness, for theirs is, the Kingdom of God.

16) Whoever tries to weaken even one of these commandments or teaches men so, he shall be called the least in the Kingdom of Heaven. **Matthew 5:19**

17) But anyone who serves and teaches them shall be called great in the Kingdom of Heaven. **Matthew 5:19**

18) Unless your righteousness exceeds that of the scribes and the Pharisees, you shall not enter the Kingdom of heaven. **Matthew 5:20**

19) Seek first the Kingdom of God and his righteousness, and all these things [food, clothing] shall be added to you. **Matthew 6:33**

20)Ask and it shall be given to you; seek and you shall find; knock and it shall be opened to you. **Matthew 7:7**

21) Not everyone who says to me, My Lord, who will enter into the Kingdom of Heaven, but he who does the will of my Father. **Matthew 7:21**

END OF SERMON ON THE MOUNT

22) A great many will come from the east and from the west, and sit down with Abraham and Issac and Jacob, in the Kingdom of Heaven. **Matthew 8:11**

23) Among those born of women there has never risen one greater than John the Baptist -- and yet even the least person in the Kingdom of Heaven is greater than he. **Matthew 11:11**

24-25) From the days of John the Baptist until now the Kingdom of Heaven has been administered by force, and only those in power control it. For all the prophets and the law prophesied until John. **Matthew 11:12**

26)...yet even the least person in the Kingdom of God is greater than he. **Luke 7:28**

27) Jesus was traveling in the cities and villages, preaching and giving good news of the Kingdom of God. **Luke 8:1**

28-29) If I [Jesus] cast out devils by the spirit of God, then the Kingdom of God has come near to you. **Matthew 12:28**

30) If I cast out devils by the finger of God, then the Kingdom of God has come near you. **Luke 11:20**

PARABLES OF THE KINGDOM OF HEAVEN

31) (1) The Kingdom of heaven is like A MAN WHO SOWED GOOD SEED in his field ...• while you pullout the tares, you might uproot the wheat. [Later] pick first the tares ...burn ...gather the wheat into my barn. **Matthew 13:37,38**

32)Such is the Kingdom of God as a man who casts seed into the ground ....When the fruit is ripe,...harvests. **Mark 4:26**

33-34) To you it is granted to know the mystery of the Kingdom of Heaven. **Matthew 13:11**

35)To you is given to know the mystery of the Kingdom of God. **Mark 4:11**

36)To you it is granted to know the mystery of the Kingdom of God. **Luke 8:10**

37-38) (2) The Kingdom of Heaven is like a **GRAIN OF MUSTARD SEED,** which a man took and sowed in his field...the smallest of all seeds…become a tree. **Matthew 13:31**

39)[The Kingdom of Heaven] is like a grain of mustard seed... **Mark 4:30-32**

40)(The Kingdom of Heaven] is like a grain of mustard seed. .. **Luke 13:18-19**

41-42) (3) The Kingdom of Heaven is like the **LEAVEN** which a woman took and buried in three measures of flour, until it was all leavened. **Matthew 13: 31**

43)[The Kingdom of Heaven] is like the leaven ...**Luke 13:21**

44) (4) The Kingdom of Heaven is like a **HIDDEN TREASURE** in a field, which a man discovered and hid, ...sold everything he had and bought that field. **Matthew 13:44**

45) (5) The Kingdom of Heaven is like a **NET,** which was thrown into the sea, and it gathered fish of every king ...good ones they put into bags, and the bad they threw away. **Matthew 13:47**

46) (6) The Kingdom of Heaven is like a man who is a householder, who brings out new and old things from his treasures. **Matthew 13:52**

47) Jesus traveled in all the towns and villages, teaching in their synagogues and preaching the gospel of the kingdom and healing every kind of sickness and disease. **Matthew 9:35**

48) [Jesus] sent them [the twelve disciples] to preach the Kingdom of God and to heal the sick. **Luke 9:2**

49) When the apostles returned •.. [Jesus] took them to a lonely place in Bethsaida. When the people found it out, they went after him. He received. them and spoke to them concerning the Kingdom of God, and he healed those in need of healing. **Luke 9:10**

50) [To Peter] I will give you the keys of the kingdom. **Matthew 16:19**

51) For whoever wishes to save his life will lose it; and whoever loses his life for my sake and the sake of MY GOSPEL [The Kingdom of Heaven is here, now]will save it. **Mark 8:35**

52-53) There are men standing here who shall not taste death till they see that the Kingdom of God has come with power. **Mark 9:1**

54) There are men who stand here who will not taste death until they see the Kingdom of Heaven. **Luke 9:27**

55-56) The disciples asked Jesus, Who is the greatest in the Kingdom of Heaven? ...Unless you change and become like little children, you shall not enter into the Kingdom of Heaven Whoever will humble himself like this child, shall be great in the Kingdom of Heaven. **Matthew 18:3-4**

57) If your eye offends you, remove it; it is better for you to enter the Kingdom of God with one eye than to have two eyes and fall into the hell of fire. **Mark 9:47**

58) The Kingdom of Heaven is like a KING WHO WANTED TO TAKE AN ACCOUNTING FROM HIS SERVANTS' Master cancelled his debt ...and that servant [did not forgive a debtor] and put him in prison ... On hearing this, the master delivered him to the scourgers until he would pay everything he owed him. **Matthew 18:23**

59) [Jesus said:] Follow me. But [the man] replied, Let me go first and bury my father [take care of until death]. [Jesus said:] Let the dead bury the dead. But you, go .and proclaim the Kingdom of God. **Luke 9**

60) No one who sets a hand to the plow and looks to what was left behind is fit for the Kingdom of God. **Luke 9:59-60**

61) [To the seventy-two disciples] Whatever town you enter say to them the Kingdom of God is at hand. [If] they do not receive you, ... say, The dust of your town that clings to our feet, even that we shake off against you. Yet know this, The Kingdom of God is at hand. **Luke 10:16**

THE GREATEST COMMANDMENT

62) Which is the greatest commandment? [In Luke: What must I do to inherit eternal life?] Love God; love your neighbor. With understanding these two commandments, you are not far from the Kingdom of Heaven. **(Deut.6:5 Lev.19:18) Matthew 22 Mark 12 Luke 10**

63) But if it is by the finger of God that (I) drive out demons, then the Kingdom of God has come upon you. **Luke 11:20**

64) Seek his kingdom and these other things will be given you besides. **Luke 12:31**

65) ...one of the guests ...said Blessed is he who will eat bread in the Kingdom of Heaven ... Jesus said, A man gave a great supper ... [invited guests did not come] ...bring in the poor, the afflicted, the maimed, and the blind. **Luke 14:15-24**

66) The Law and the Prophets lasted until John; but from then on the good word of the Kingdom of God is preached... **Luke 16:16**

67-68) The Kingdom of God can not be observed, and no one will announce it... For THE KINGDOM OF GOD is within you. **Luke 17:20**

69) Some [Eunuchs] make themselves that way for the Kingdom of Heaven. **Matthew 19:12**

70-71) For the Kingdom of Heaven is for such as these children. **Matthew 19:13-15, Mark 10:15-17, Luke 18:15-17**

72-73) Whoever does not receive the Kingdom of Heaven like a little child shall not enter it. **Mark 10:15, Luke 18:17**

74-75) It will be hard for one who is rich to enter the Kingdom of Heaven. **Matthew 19:13-15, Mark 10:15-17,Luke 18:15-17**

76) [Jesus said:] Children, how hard it is to enter the Kingdom of God!
Mark 10:24

77-78) It. is easier for a rope [camel: Aramaic word gamia means rope and camel] to pass through the eye of a needle than for one who is rich to enter the Kingdom of God. **Matthew 19:24**

79) Then Peter said, we have given up our possessions and followed you. (Jesus said to them;) There is no one who has given up house or wife or brothers or parents or children for the sake of the Kingdom of God who will not receive back an overabundant return in this present age and eternal life in the age to come.
Luke 18:29

80) MANY WHO ARE FIRST WILL BE LAST, AND THE LAST WILL BE FIRST. The Kingdom of Heaven is like a landowner who went out at dawn to hire laborers. After agreeing with them for the usual daily wage, he sent them into his vineyard .... he went out .[twice more and hired labors at different times.] ... Beginning with the last and ending with the first each received the usual daily wage. The first to be hired expected more wages. The landowner said, "I am not cheating you. You agreed for the usual daily wage. Am I not free to do as I wish with my own money? Are you envious because I am generous?" Thus the last will be first, and the first will be last. **Matthew 20:28**

81) [Jesus said:] Tax collectors and prostitutes [who believed John] are entering the Kingdom of God before you [who did not believe John] . **Matthew 21:31**

82) [Jesus said:] The Kingdom of God will be taken from you [who do not respect the Son] and given to a people that will produce its fruit. **Matthew 21:43-44**

83) The Kingdom of Heaven may be likened to a king who gave a wedding feast for his son... invited guest refused to come ... a second time he sent servants who were killed by those invited ... Go out into the main roads and invite to the feast whomever you find... they found bad and good ... The king found a man not dressed in a wedding garment ...cast him out. Many are invited-but few are chosen. **Matthew 22:1-8**

84) [Jesus said:] Woe to you, scribes and Pharisees, you hypocrites. You shut off the Kingdom of Heaven before men, for you do not enter into it yourself and do not permit those who would to enter.
Matthew 23:13

85) This gospel of the Kingdom will be preached throughout the world. **Matthew 24:14**

86) [Jesus said:] Consider the fig tree and all the other trees. When their buds burst open, you see for yourselves and know that summer is now near. In the same way, when you see these things [signs] happening, know that the Kingdom of God is near. **Luke 21:29-31**

87) The Kingdom of Heaven will be like ten bridesmaids…five took oil for their lamps and five foolish ones did not. When it was announced that the bridegroom was coming, the foolish ones asked the other five for some oil. There would not be enough oil for them, so when they went to purchase oil, the bridegroom came, and those five who were ready, entered with him into the banqueting house and the door was locked. To the foolish five, the bridegroom said, "I do not know you. " BE ALERT. YOU DO NOT KNOW THE DAY NOR THE HOUR. **Matthew 25:3**

88) When the hour carne, [Jesus] took his place at table, with the apostles. He said, I have eagerly desired to eat this Passover with you before I suffer, for I tell you, I shall not eat it [again] until there is fulfillment in the Kingdom of God. (Fulfilled = all people will recline at table in the Kingdom of God.) Take this, and share it, for I tell you from this time on I shall not drink of the fruit of the vine until the Kingdom of God comes. **Luke 22:15**

89) My kingdom is not of this world. **John 18:36**

90)From now on I shall not drink this fruit of the vine until the day when I drink it with you new in the Kingdom of My Father. **Matthew 26:29**

91)I shall not drink again the fruit of the vine until the day when I drink it new in the Kingdom of God.
Mark 14:25

92-93) Joseph of Arimathea, a distinguished member of the council, who was himself awaiting the Kingdom of God **Mark 15:43**

94) He came from the Jewish town of Arimathea and was awaiting the Kingdom of God. **Luke 23:51**

THE WAY TO THE KINGDOM OF HEAVEN

1) Jesus came to preach the good news of the Kingdom of Heaven. **Mark 1:14**

2) Repent for the Kingdom of Heaven is here and now. **Matthew 4:17**

3) SEEK FIRST the Kingdom of God and his righteousness and all your needs shall be provided. **Matthew 6:33 Luke 12:31**

4) The Kingdom of Heaven is within you. **Luke 17:21**

5) The Kingdom of Heaven is not of this world. **John 18:36**

6) You must be childlike to enter the Kingdom of Heaven. **Mark 10:15**

7) You must be unattached to earthly possessions to enter the Kingdom of Heaven. **Matthew 19:23, Mark 10:45**

8) Your are near the Kingdom of Heaven when you love God with all your heart, mind, soul, and strength and love your neighbor as yourself, and act neighborly. **Matthew 22:39, Mark 12:31, Luke 10:25-37**

9) The Kingdom of Heaven is all encompassing like a tiny mustard seed that becomes a great tree or the leaven in flour making it all leaven. **Matthew 13:31-33**

10) The Kingdom of Heaven is like a pearl of great price which a man finds and then sells everything to purchase it. **Matthew 13:46**

###

ABOUT THE AUTHOR

Karl F. Hollenbach was born in 1925 in Louisville, Kentucky. He received his B.A. and M. Ed. from the University of Louisville. His esoteric and metaphysical articles have been published in Japan and England as well as the United States. He and his artist wife live on Dunsinane Hill Farm near Fort Knox, Kentucky.

Additional information about the author may be found at http://BooksAuthorsAndArtists.com and on the Books, Authors and Artists Facebook page at https://www.facebook.com/BooksAuthorsAndArtists

Also by Karl F. Hollenbach

A JOURNEY TO THE FOUR KINGDOMS

ANECDOTES AND SPECIAL NOTES

SCROOGE AND MARLEY

PATTON: MANY LIVES, MANY BATTLES

MANSIONS OF THE MOON (formerly ERICIUS)

FRANCIS ROSICROSS

HANDBOOK – APPLYING METAPHYSICAL PRINCIPLES IN TEACHING

THE GREAT HAWK

THE RIGHTEOUS ROGUE

THRICE TOLD TALES